NFL TODAY

THE STORY OF THE
DENVER BRONCOS

THE STORY OF THE DENVER BRONCOS

TYLER OMOTH

CREATIVE EDUCATION

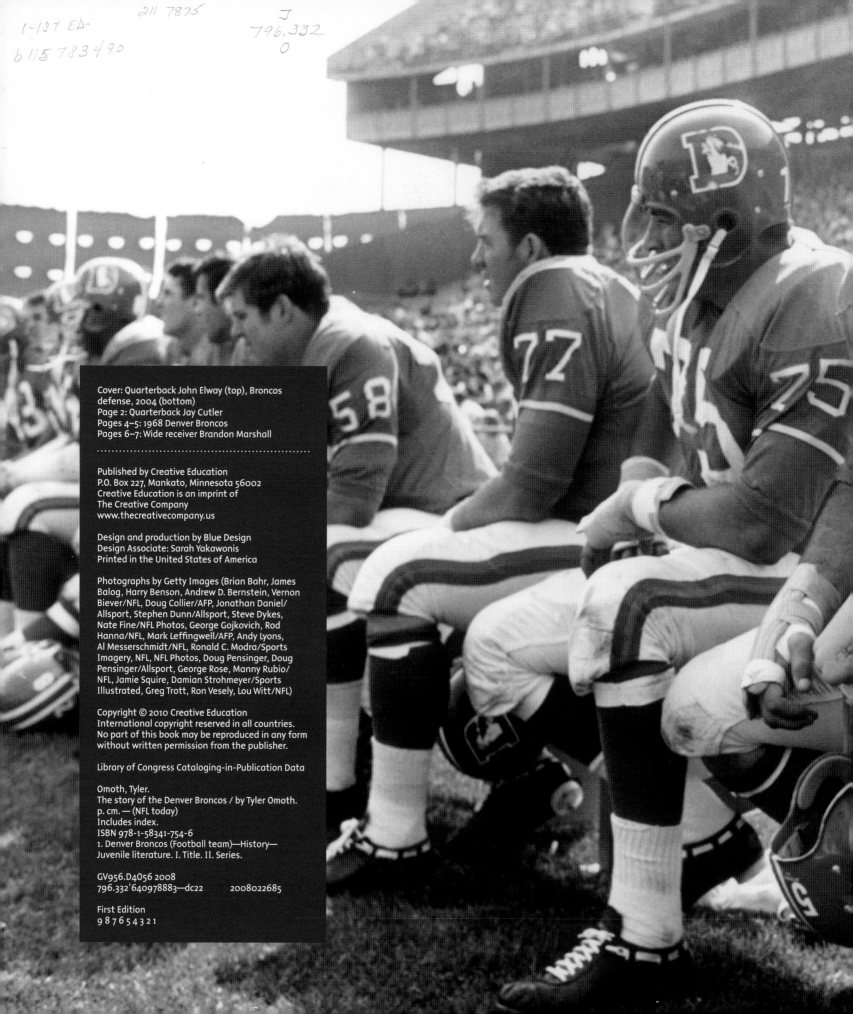

Cover: Quarterback John Elway (top), Broncos
defense, 2004 (bottom)
Page 2: Quarterback Jay Cutler
Pages 4–5: 1968 Denver Broncos
Pages 6–7: Wide receiver Brandon Marshall

....

Published by Creative Education
P.O. Box 227, Mankato, Minnesota 56002
Creative Education is an imprint of
The Creative Company
www.thecreativecompany.us

Design and production by Blue Design
Design Associate: Sarah Yakawonis
Printed in the United States of America

Photographs by Getty Images (Brian Bahr, James
Balog, Harry Benson, Andrew D. Bernstein, Vernon
Biever/NFL, Doug Collier/AFP, Jonathan Daniel/
Allsport, Stephen Dunn/Allsport, Steve Dykes,
Nate Fine/NFL Photos, George Gojkovich, Rod
Hanna/NFL, Mark Leffingwell/AFP, Andy Lyons,
Al Messerschmidt/NFL, Ronald C. Modra/Sports
Imagery, NFL, NFL Photos, Doug Pensinger, Doug
Pensinger/Allsport, George Rose, Manny Rubio/
NFL, Jamie Squire, Damian Strohmeyer/Sports
Illustrated, Greg Trott, Ron Vesely, Lou Witt/NFL)

Library of Congress Cataloging-in-Publication Data

Omoth, Tyler.
The story of the Denver Broncos / by Tyler Omoth.
p. cm. — (NFL today)
Includes index.
ISBN 978-1-58341-754-6
1. Denver Broncos (Football team)—History—
Juvenile literature. I. Title. II. Series.

GV956.D4056 2008
796.332'640978883—dc22   2008022685

First Edition
9 8 7 6 5 4 3 2 1

CONTENTS

ON THE SIDELINES

MEET THE BRONCOS

AN UGLY BEGINNING

X

Situated a mile above sea level, Denver is one of America's most beautiful cities and busiest tourist destinations. Denver started out small, as a supply town for the quickly growing Colorado gold-mining camps in the mid-1800s. By the 1950s, Denver was a truly rich city. In addition to its booming businesses, the "Mile-High City" boasted stunning scenery, clean air, and famous ski resorts. One thing that was missing, however, was a professional football team.

In 1959, Denver businessman Bob Howsam purchased a franchise in the newly formed American Football League (AFL), thereby becoming a founding member of "The Foolish Club" (a nickname bestowed on the original AFL team owners by their National Football League, or NFL, counterparts, who thought that the new league was doomed to failure). In an attempt to generate interest in the new club, Howsam announced a public "name-the-team" contest in 1960. The winning suggestion was Broncos, a reference to the bucking horses in the rodeos common in Colorado.

The Broncos came bucking right out of the gate by winning the very first AFL game, defeating the Boston Patriots 13–10. After that, though, Denver struggled. Fans saw some great performances by ballhawking safety Austin "Goose" Gonsoulin (who intercepted four passes in one game), veteran

X Due to its mountain location, Denver poses a unique challenge to NFL players and other athletes; its high elevation means the air contains less oxygen, causing players to tire more quickly.

quarterback Frank Tripucka, and sure-handed end Lionel Taylor, but the Broncos ended their first season with a 4–9–1 record, last in the eight-team AFL.

To make matters worse, the Broncos had the ugliest uniforms in the league. The team's general manager had tried to save money by buying used college uniforms. The Broncos' brown jerseys and yellow pants were bad enough, but the worst part of the uniform was the vertically striped stockings, which were so hideous that the players offered to buy their own.

After Denver slipped to 3–11 in its second season, the team hired a new coach named Jack Faulkner. In an effort to light a fire under his young club, Coach Faulkner changed the team uniforms. The updated look seemed to help, as the new orange-and-blue Broncos leaped to a 7–2 start in 1962. Even though the team stumbled late in the season, fan attendance at home games doubled, and Faulkner was named the AFL Coach of the Year.

Unfortunately, no other Broncos season would be that successful during the rest of the 1960s. The team would be led by five different coaches during the decade, but none would guide the Broncos to a winning record. Although Denver would feature such brilliant players as running back Cookie Gilchrist and receiver Al Denson during these years, it would finish its opening decade with a collective 39–97–4 record— the worst of any of the original AFL teams.

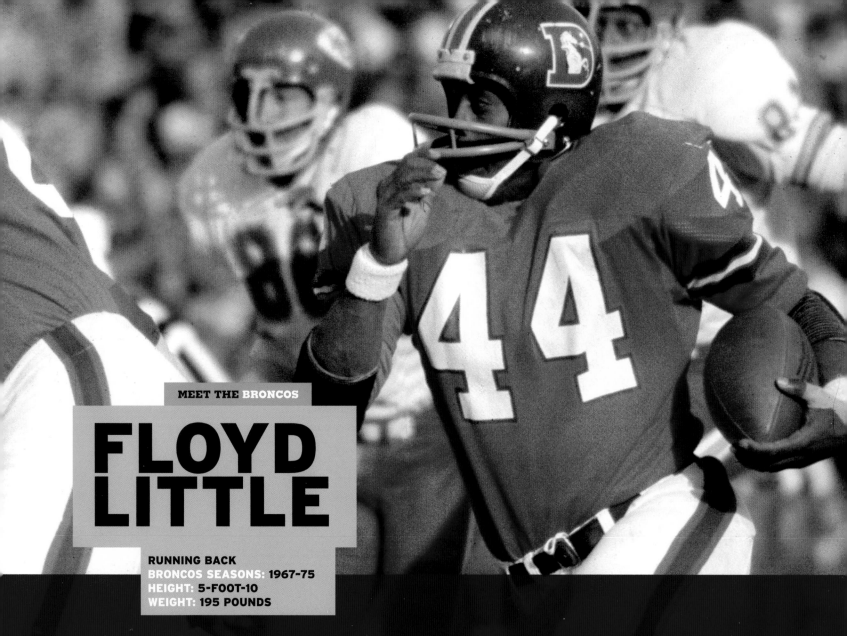

FLOYD LITTLE

RUNNING BACK
BRONCOS SEASONS: 1967-75
HEIGHT: 5-FOOT-10
WEIGHT: 195 POUNDS

Orange is a color that suited Floyd Little well. He first donned it as a three-time All-American halfback for the Syracuse University Orangemen, then he pulled on a new orange jersey when he was drafted by the Denver Broncos in 1967. From the moment he signed with the Broncos, Little was known in Denver simply as "The Franchise." True to his last name, Little was a bit small at just 5-foot-10 and less than 200 pounds, but what he lacked in size he made up for in field vision and quick moves. Those moves also made Little a crucial part of the Broncos' special-teams unit as a dangerous kick returner. In 1973, The Franchise helped the Broncos attain their first winning season as they finished 7–5–2. Lou Saban, who coached the Broncos and then the Buffalo Bills, admired Little's passion. "Floyd has a driving force that no one I know can equal," he said. "He is a man. That's about as much as you can say about anybody." When the Broncos established their "Ring of Fame" in 1984, Little was one of the first inductees.

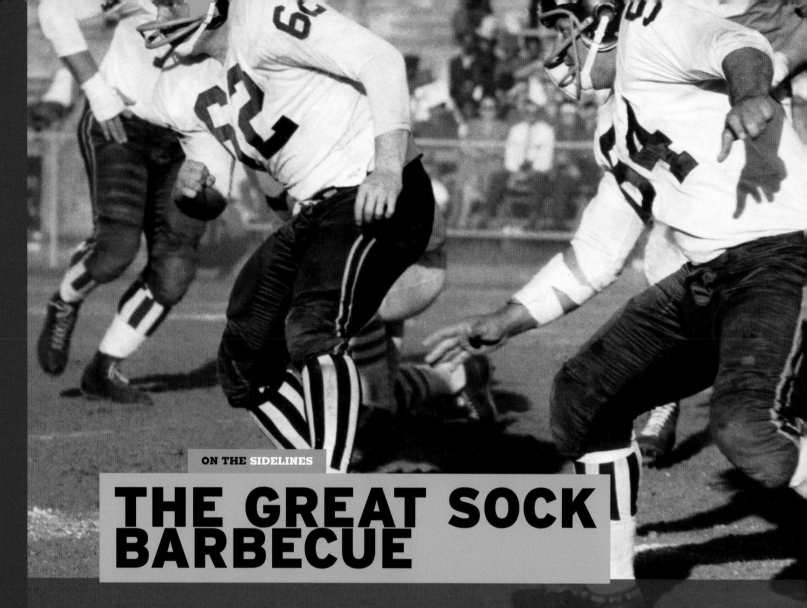

ON THE SIDELINES

THE GREAT SOCK BARBECUE

For decades, the Denver Broncos have been closely, and proudly, connected to the color orange. But during their first two seasons, they weren't so lucky. Short on money, the team's general manager, Dean Griffing, chose to buy used uniforms featuring yellow jerseys with numbers that matched the team's brown pants. The uniforms were ugly, but the accompanying striped socks were historically bad. After Denver went a combined 7–20–1 in its first two seasons, Jack Faulkner was brought in as the new head coach and general manager. Hoping to change their luck, the team bought new uniforms and introduced the slogan "There's lots new in '62!" Then Faulkner held a public burning of what had become the symbol of those first two dismal years: the hated socks. In front of more than 8,000 fans gathered in Denver's Bears Stadium, Broncos players marched past a replica of the Olympic flame and tossed their hated striped socks into the fire. Defensive tackle Bud McFadden echoed the thoughts of many of his teammates when he said, "They were the most ridiculous [socks] I ever saw in my life."

Remarkably, despite their losing ways, the Broncos' popularity kept climbing. Starting in 1970 (the year the AFL merged with the NFL) and continuing for three decades, every home game would be sold out. One of the reasons for this amazing support was Denver's ability to attract exciting stars such as running back Floyd Little.

In 1967, the Broncos paid the then huge sum of $130,000 for Little, who had been a three-time All-American at Syracuse University. When he gained only 381 rushing yards his rookie year, disappointed fans called him the "$130,000 Lemon." Then, in 1968, the franchise reached a turning point. The team adopted new uniforms with a helmet that featured a bucking bronco inside of a capital *D*. And jeers turned to cheers as Little—running behind linemen Larry Kaminski, Bob Young, and Tom Beer—began to tear through opposing defenses. "I remember one play in one game late in that 1968 season," Little later recalled. "It wasn't the length of the run, which was short, or the game, which was just another game, but it was the execution of the play. It was perfect.... All of a sudden, all the pieces of our jigsaw puzzle were falling into place." Seating in Denver's Bears Stadium was increased to 51,706 seats, and before the final game of the season, the Broncos' home was renamed Mile High Stadium.

Despite Little's optimism, the Broncos continued to come up short in the standings, finishing 5–8–1 in both 1969

and 1970. After starting out 1971 with a 2–6–1 record, general manager and head coach Lou Saban resigned, and the Broncos finished 4–9–1. Under yet another new coach, John Ralston, Denver maintained its losing ways in 1972 with a 5–9 record. Despite it all, Broncos fans continued to show up and support their team.

After several years of disappointment, the Denver faithful finally began to feel optimistic as the 1973 season rolled around. Thanks to quarterback Charley Johnson and players such as Little and deep-threat receiver Haven Moses, fans had good reason to be hopeful. The Broncos finished 1973 with a winning record for the first time in franchise history, going 7–5–2. In 1974, the team expanded the stadium's seating capacity again—this time to 75,000—to accommodate the rapidly growing demand for tickets as the Broncos finished with their second straight winning record. Unfortunately, the next year, Denver fell to 6–8 in what proved to be Little's last season. When the player known as "The Franchise" retired in 1975, the team retired his number 44 jersey along with him.

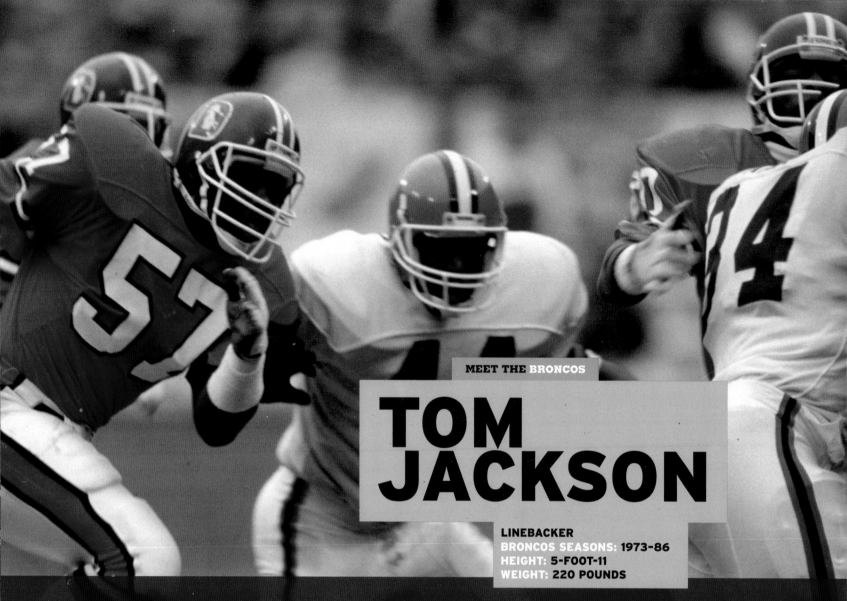

TOM JACKSON

LINEBACKER
BRONCOS SEASONS: 1973-86
HEIGHT: 5-FOOT-11
WEIGHT: 220 POUNDS

From the time he was a kid, Tom Jackson was told that he was too small to be a successful football player. Even after a terrific college career at the University of Louisville, he was not chosen until the fourth round of the 1973 NFL Draft. Both intelligent and dedicated, the player who was supposed to be too little became a crucial part of Denver's "Orange Crush" defense of the mid-1970s. In the 1977 playoffs, the Broncos' first postseason appearance, Jackson helped his team defeat the Pittsburgh Steelers with two interceptions and a fumble recovery. His dedication made him exceptionally popular with fans, and his teammates voted him the Broncos' "Most Inspirational Player" for six consecutive seasons. "I loved to practice," he said in an interview after retiring. "I loved lying there in a puddle of sweat, exhausted and knowing that I was preparing myself as best I could to be successful on the weekend." After a 14-year NFL career, Jackson put his football knowledge to use by becoming one of the most respected NFL analysts on television.

BRONCOMANIA

x -

The hiring of Denver's eighth head coach, Robert "Red" Miller, in 1977 signaled the start of a new era. That era was dubbed "Broncomania" due to the wild enthusiasm that filled Mile High Stadium for each Broncos home game. Coach Miller helped trigger that excitement before the 1977 season by announcing, "The Broncos will make Denver proud. We're not scared of anyone. We can beat any team."

Miller's players backed up his words, winning the franchise's first American Football Conference (AFC) West Division title with a 12–2 record. Led by veteran quarterback Craig Morton, Denver's offense was anything but explosive. But with a defense featuring huge linemen Rubin Carter and Lyle Alzado and fearless linebackers Randy Gradishar and Tom Jackson, Denver didn't need to score many points to win. Nicknamed the "Orange Crush" on account of its orange home jerseys and physical style of play, the Denver defense was one of the NFL's most dominant.

When the defending Super Bowl champion Oakland Raiders arrived at Mile High Stadium for the 1977 AFC Championship Game, all they could see was orange. Denver fans went wild as the Orange Crush held Oakland to a first-half field goal, and the Broncos won 20–17 to advance to Super Bowl XII. Unfortunately, the Broncos fell just short of a

X Running back Rob Lytle gained distinction by scoring the first Super Bowl touchdown (in Super Bowl XII) ever by a Denver player.

world championship, losing 27–10 to an opportunistic Dallas Cowboys defense that recovered four Denver fumbles and intercepted the ball four times.

With its crushing defense still dominating opponents, Denver powered its way to the playoffs again in 1978 with a 10–6 record. However, the Broncos defense wasn't enough to suppress the Pittsburgh Steelers' powerful offense in the postseason, and Denver was routed 33–10. In 1979, another 10–6 record earned the team a Wild Card berth into the playoffs. This time it was the Houston Oilers that knocked

X Although his reputation would later be tarnished by admissions of steroid use, lineman Lyle Alzado was a feared defensive force during his eight seasons in Denver.

THE ORANGE CRUSH

Great team units often earn great nicknames. In the late 1960s and early '70s, that was especially true with dominant defenses in the NFL. The stingy defense of the Pittsburgh Steelers was dubbed "The Steel Curtain." The ferocious attack of the Minnesota Vikings' defensive line earned it the nickname "Purple People Eaters." So when the 1977 Denver Broncos defense led the AFC in fewest points, yards, and rushing yards allowed per game, it seemed only fitting that it should have a nickname of its own. While being named after a popular soft drink, Orange Crush, may not seem too intimidating, it was certainly appropriate. The Denver defense, wearing its bright orange jerseys, consistently crushed opposing offenses with the fearsome play of defensive linemen such as Lyle Alzado and Rubin Carter and linebackers Randy Gradishar and Tom Jackson. "The Orange Crush was a nickname we enjoyed," defensive back Billy Thompson recalled. "It was a signature time in Broncos history because we moved from being a team that wasn't respectable to a team that had a chance to win."

the Broncos from Super Bowl contention, topping Denver 13–7. Those seasons cemented the Broncos' legacy as one of the NFL's finest teams of the late '70s, even though a world championship remained just out of reach.

After Denver faded to 8–8 in 1980, Coach Miller was replaced by Dan Reeves. A man with extensive Super Bowl experience, Reeves had played or coached in five Super Bowls with the Dallas Cowboys. When Reeves led the Broncos to an improved 10–6 mark his first year, Denver fans began dreaming of Super Bowl glory once again. But many Broncos greats of the '70s had gotten old or moved on, and Denver lacked a true star to guide it to success in the postseason.

That changed in 1983. That year's NFL Draft produced a number of quarterbacks who would become legendary stars, but the Broncos got the one every team wanted most: Stanford University standout John Elway. An All-American with a cannon for an arm, Elway would become the decisive leader that the Broncos had been lacking.

After Denver made him the NFL's highest-paid rookie, Elway proved his worth by coolly leading the Broncos to the playoffs in 1983. Then, in 1984, the young quarterback guided Denver to the AFC West title with a 13–3 mark. Whether he was launching a deep pass, firing up his teammates, or scrambling

In the 10 years (1983–1992) that Denver had coach Dan Reeves on the sidelines and John Elway under center, the Broncos suffered just 1 losing season and made the playoffs 6 times. **X**

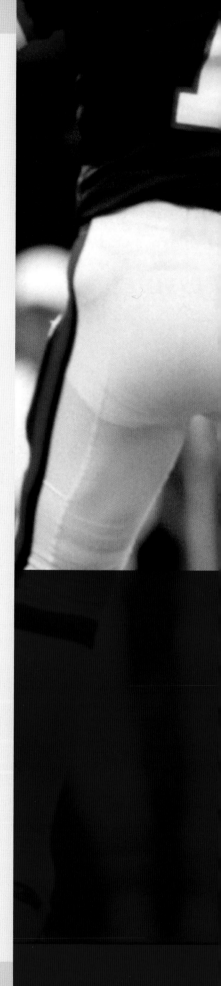

for a big gain, Elway expected a lot from himself. "My goal is to beat [Hall of Fame Pittsburgh Steelers quarterback] Terry Bradshaw," Elway said. "He won the Super Bowl four times. I want to win five."

The Broncos made quick exits from the playoffs in 1983 and 1984. Although the team missed the playoffs in 1985, Elway put on a great show, throwing for 3,891 yards and 22 touchdowns, with many of those passes going to receiver Vance Johnson. That was just the start of one of the most remarkable careers in NFL history. In all, the quarterback in the number 7 jersey would spend 16 seasons in the Mile-High City, passing for more than 3,000 yards in 12 of them.

KARL MECKLENBURG

LINEBACKER
BRONCOS SEASONS: 1983-94
HEIGHT: 6-FOOT-3
WEIGHT: 240 POUNDS

Karl Mecklenburg's NFL career is one of the great Cinderella stories in league history. He was a walk-on player at the University of Minnesota, and in 1983, he waited until the 12th round of the NFL Draft before the Broncos selected him. The 310th overall pick in the draft, Mecklenburg went on to earn six Pro Bowl selections. After he spent one season at defensive end, the Broncos chose to capitalize on his versatile skills by moving him around a lot. Although Mecklenburg is primarily remembered as a linebacker, his athleticism encouraged coaches to put him at seven different positions on defense, many times lining him up at each one in a single game. Wherever he lined up, he was a devastating tackler and a fearsome pass rusher, notching a career high of 13 sacks in 1985. Mecklenburg's defensive leadership helped the Broncos get to three Super Bowls during his career, although they came up short in each one. As of 2008, he remained a popular figure in Colorado, dedicating much of his time to coaching the Kent Denver High School football team and helping local charities.

THE ELWAY ERA

In the late 1980s, new defensive stars emerged in Denver, including linebacker Karl Mecklenburg and safety Dennis Smith. Yet it was Elway who remained the driving force behind the Broncos. As he led the team into the playoffs in 1986, 1987, and 1989, he became known as a "comeback king" due to his knack for rallying the Broncos on game-winning drives late in the fourth quarter.

One such drive took place in the AFC Championship Game after the 1986 season. Trailing the Cleveland Browns 20–13 with just five and a half minutes left in the game, the Broncos got the ball on their own two-yard line. Facing a tough Browns defense, a rowdy Cleveland crowd, and a stiff wind, Elway completed one pressure-packed pass after another to drive Denver the length of the field for the tying touchdown. Broncos kicker Rich Karlis, who famously always kicked with a bare foot, then booted a field goal for a 23–20 overtime victory, earning Denver a berth in Super Bowl XXI against the New York Giants. Unfortunately for Denver fans, the Giants were loaded with talent that year and crushed the Broncos, 39–20.

The Broncos rebounded from that loss by marching right back to the Super Bowl in 1987 and 1989. Denver fans were again left brokenhearted by the outcomes, though. After the Broncos were crushed by the Washington Redskins, 42–10,

Although the Broncos lost Super Bowl XXI, quarterback John Elway gave a terrific performance on football's biggest stage, passing for 304 yards and scrambling for another 27. **X**------

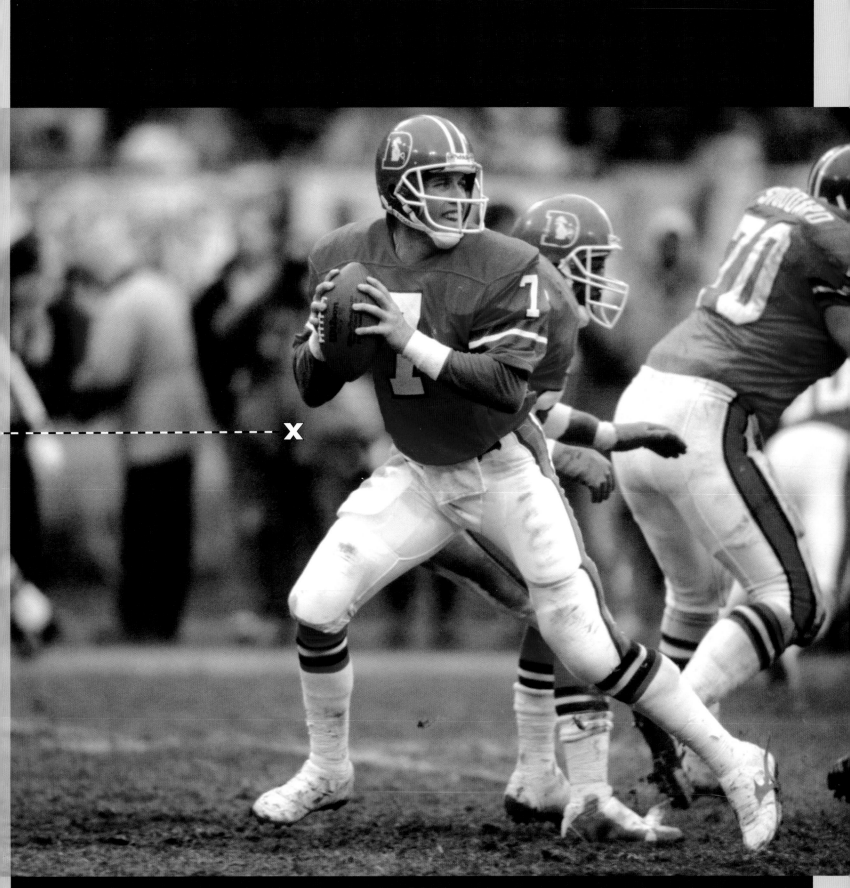

X

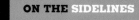

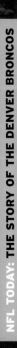
ON THE SIDELINES

CELEBRATING ORANGE

When the Denver Broncos kicked off the 1973 season, the team still had not enjoyed a winning season in its 13-year history. Broncos fans remained true to their team, though, and showed their support by renewing 47,800 season tickets for that season. After starting out 2–3, the Broncos were slated to take on the Oakland Raiders in front of a prime-time national television audience on Monday Night Football on October 22. In honor of the team's first appearance on the Monday Night stage, Denver mayor Bill McNichols declared the day "Orange Monday." The Broncos faithful were encouraged to wear orange and blue all day and show their support for the team throughout the entire city. The game marked a significant turning point, as the fans cheered the Broncos on to a 23–23 tie versus the powerful Raiders, capped by kicker Jim Turner's 35-yard field goal. Although the Broncos weren't able to walk away with the victory, the game began the team's first-ever six-game unbeaten streak and put Denver on its way to its first winning season in franchise history.

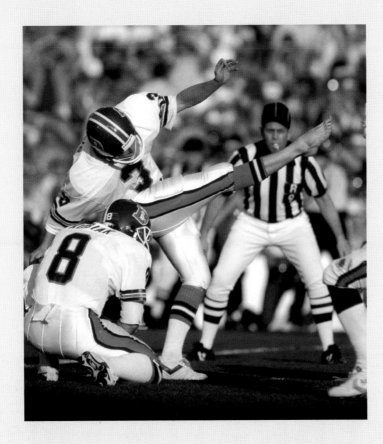

and the San Francisco 49ers, 55–10, some critics wondered if Denver would ever win the big game. But even as the team put together some mediocre seasons in the early 1990s, Elway and new stars such as tight end Shannon Sharpe and hard-hitting safety Steve Atwater gave fans hope.

In 1995, the Broncos made two key moves that would finally take them to the top. First, they hired Mike Shanahan—the offensive coordinator for the 49ers team that had beaten the Broncos in Super Bowl XXIV—as the franchise's 11th head coach. Then, in the 1995 NFL Draft,

X Rich Karlis set or tied several NFL records with his barefooted kicking style, including field goals in a game (seven, set in 1989).

the Broncos found a hidden gem. With the 196th pick, they selected University of Georgia running back Terrell Davis. Called "T. D." by his teammates, Davis quickly gave the Broncos a deadly rushing attack.

In 1996, as linemen Gary Zimmerman and Brian Habib paved the way, Davis charged for 1,538 yards. Behind this sensational effort, the Broncos went 13–3 and won their division before losing to the Jacksonville Jaguars in a playoff upset. Denver dug deeper in 1997 as Davis exploded for

X Veteran tackle Gary Zimmerman helped the Broncos lead the NFL in total yards in 1996 and 1997 with his outstanding blocking.

Terrell Davis was in peak form in Super Bowl XXXII after the 1997 season, rumbling through the Packers defense for 157 yards and 3 touchdowns. **X**

1,750 yards on the season, and young receiver Rod Smith emerged as a big-play threat to help Denver reach its fifth Super Bowl. This time, Denver faced the defending Super Bowl champion Green Bay Packers.

With the game tied 24–24 in the fourth quarter, Elway led yet another sensational drive, marching Denver down the field. Then, with less than two minutes remaining, Davis plunged into the end zone to finally give the Broncos their first world championship. "I'm so proud and happy that we could win this for Denver fans and for John," said Davis. "John Elway has meant everything to this franchise, and it's so great to see him finally get what he deserves."

Denver fans found more reasons for celebration the next season. After Davis became the fourth running back in NFL history to rush for more than 2,000 yards in a season, the Broncos galloped back to the Super Bowl. In what turned out to be Elway's farewell performance, the Hall of Fame quarterback passed for 336 yards in a 34–19 victory over the Atlanta Falcons. After the game, Elway announced his retirement, ending his brilliant career while on top of the football world.

After Elway rode off into the sunset, young and inexperienced quarterback Brian Griese assumed command

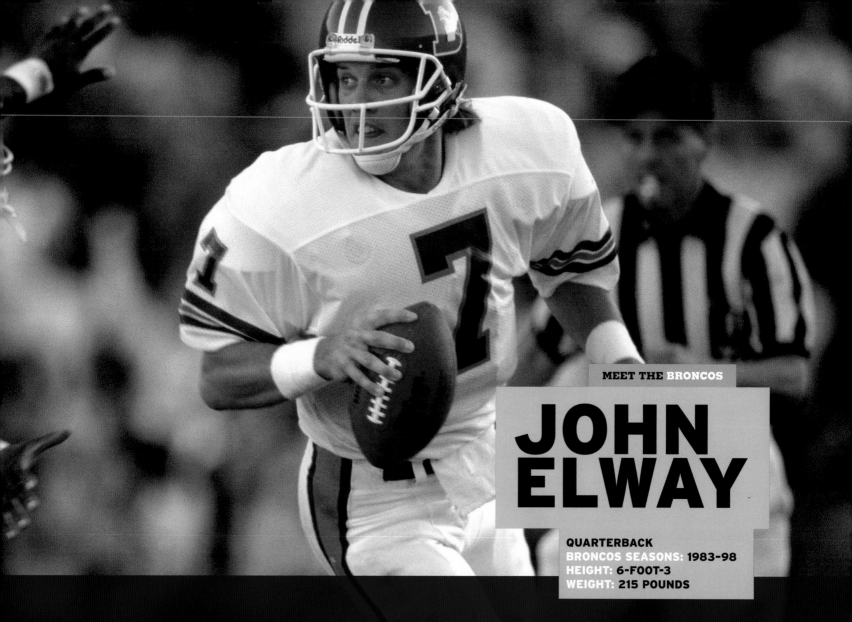

JOHN ELWAY

QUARTERBACK
BRONCOS SEASONS: 1983-98
HEIGHT: 6-FOOT-3
WEIGHT: 215 POUNDS

When time was running out and the Broncos needed to score, John Elway was at his best. Although he had a powerful passing arm and elusive scrambling ability, he was best known for his ability to rally his team late in games. In fact, as of 2009, Elway held an NFL record with 47 fourth-quarter, game-winning or game-tying drives. In the 1986 AFC title game, he led his team on a 98-yard comeback drive to help beat the Cleveland Browns with a legendary rally that is still known simply as "The Drive." Although he was one of the most respected quarterbacks in the league for more than a decade, Elway's resumé wasn't complete until Super Bowl XXXII, after the 1997 season, when the Broncos won the first of two consecutive Super Bowls behind his leadership. "The thing that was so impressive to me was the concentration level and the poise in thriving on pressure," said Broncos coach Mike Shanahan. "He knew and believed that he was so prepared, so physically in shape, that if he was put in that situation, he would win."

of the offense and did an admirable job, passing for more than 3,000 yards in his first season under center. After posting a disappointing 6–10 record in 1999, Griese and the Broncos opened the new century in fine style by going 11–5, though they lost to the Baltimore Ravens, 21–3, in a Wild Card playoff game.

NEW STARS STEP UP

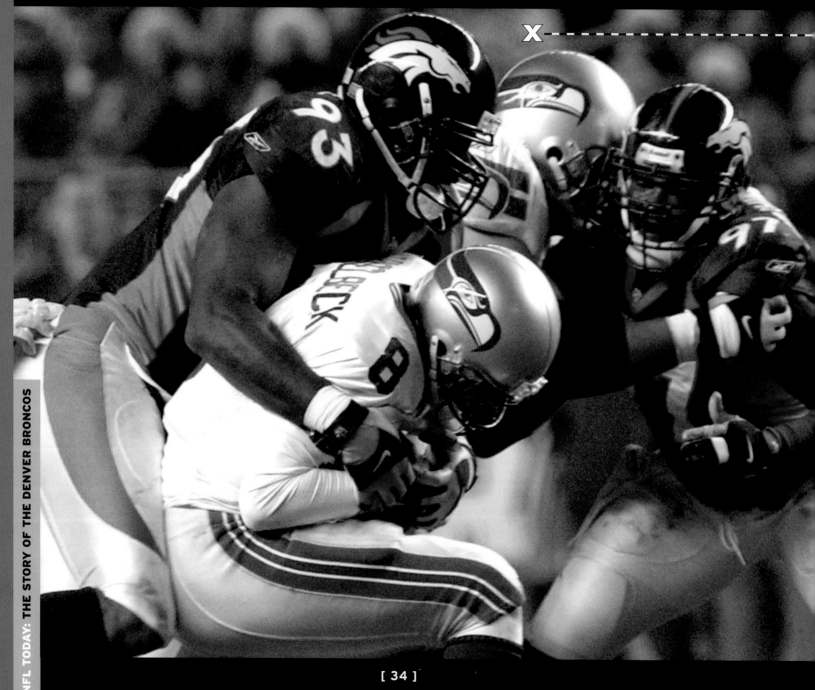

Longtime Broncos defensive end Trevor Pryce (number 93) had the best season of his career in 2000, notching 12 sacks, forcing 2 fumbles, and scoring his first NFL touchdown.

In 2001, the Broncos left their longtime home of Mile High Stadium and moved into the newly constructed Invesco Field at Mile High. That year, Terrell Davis suffered a knee injury that limited him to just eight games; sadly, he would never be able to return to form as an NFL running back. After an 8–8 finish in 2001, the team improved to 9–7 in 2002. Both seasons were marred by inconsistent play and ended with the Broncos outside the playoff picture.

By 2003, Denver had two new offensive leaders. The first was former Arizona Cardinals quarterback Jake "The Snake" Plummer, whose confidence, quick feet, and knack for orchestrating comeback victories reminded many fans of Elway. The second was young running back Clinton Portis, who had delighted fans and inspired teammates by rushing for 1,508 yards and earning Offensive Rookie of the Year honors in 2002. "He's a true home-run threat," said Shannon Sharpe. "That's something none of the guys we had before could say."

With defensive end Trevor Pryce taking down opposing

SHANNON SHARPE

TIGHT END
BRONCOS SEASONS: 1990–99, 2002–03
HEIGHT: 6-FOOT-2
WEIGHT: 228 POUNDS

When Shannon Sharpe was on the football field, everyone knew it. One of the most notorious (and comedic) trash talkers in NFL history, he was also a vital part of the Broncos' championship-caliber offense in both 1997 and 1998. Drafted as a wide receiver, Sharpe played very little early in his first season except on special teams. Because of his size, he was used as a tight end during practices. Once the Denver coaching staff realized that he had a knack for getting open and catching passes from that position, they gave him his chance. The rest is history. Sharpe became quarterback John Elway's favorite target in tough situations and developed a reputation as a fearless pass catcher unafraid of crushing hits from linebackers. After a 14-year career, he retired as the NFL's all-time leader in receptions and receiving yards among tight ends. "I've always liked to talk, and it's who I am," he said at his retirement. After he hung up his cleats, Sharpe used his gift for gab as an NFL analyst on *The NFL Today* pre-game show on CBS.

quarterbacks and tackling machine Al Wilson manning the middle linebacker spot, the Broncos defense ranked among the AFC's best in 2003. On the offensive side of the ball, Portis topped his rookie campaign by rumbling for 1,591 yards, helping the Broncos go 10–6 and earn a spot in the playoffs as a Wild Card team. Unfortunately, the same Indianapolis Colts team that Denver had defeated in the season's final game to lock down their playoff berth proved to be too much for the Broncos in the postseason, crushing Denver 41–10.

Hoping to strengthen their defense, the Broncos then traded Portis to the Washington Redskins for Champ Bailey,

X A future Hall-of-Famer, cornerback Champ Bailey combined the toughness of a linebacker with the sure hands of a wide receiver.

arguably the NFL's best coverage cornerback. In the offensive backfield, meanwhile, newcomer Reuben Droughns picked up where Portis had left off, rushing for 1,240 yards. Denver posted a 10–6 record and once again met the Colts in the playoffs. And, once again, the Colts came out on top in a blowout, this time 49–24.

In 2005, Denver took its rushing attack—which had long been recognized as one of the most consistently powerful in the NFL—to a whole new level with a two-headed backfield consisting of Mike Anderson and Tatum Bell. Anderson led the team with 1,014 rushing yards, but Bell was right behind him with 921 yards. Thanks to this dominant rushing duo and an opportunistic defense, the Broncos put together the second-best record in the AFC at 13–3. After defeating the defending champion New England Patriots in the playoffs, the Broncos hosted the Steelers in the AFC Championship Game. Sadly, Plummer committed four turnovers, and the Steelers won 34–17.

After the Broncos' offense performed inconsistently in 2006, Coach Shanahan decided to replace Plummer with strong-armed rookie quarterback Jay Cutler. Cutler held his own as the team's playoff hopes came down to the final game of the season against the San Francisco

THE DRIVE

It was the fourth quarter of the 1986 AFC Championship Game. The Cleveland Browns were leading the visiting Denver Broncos by a score of 20–13. After a botched kickoff return, Elway and the Broncos lined up at their own 2-yard line with 5:32 left on the game clock, beginning what would eventually become known simply as "The Drive." During the 15-play drive, running back Sammy Winder ran the ball 3 times for a total of 8 yards and caught 1 pass. Elway twice had to scramble for yards to keep the drive alive. He went to the air 9 times, hitting receivers Steve Watson and Mark Jackson and running back Steve Sewell for 5 passes, including a 5-yard touchdown strike to Jackson to tie the game with 31 seconds remaining. The Drive kept the Broncos in the game and gave them the chance they needed to win it with a field goal in overtime. "Being human," wide receiver Vance Johnson said afterwards, "you tend to doubt yourself at times. But John never seemed to doubt anything at the end."

MIKE SHANAHAN

COACH
BRONCOS SEASONS: 1995-2008

Between 1995 and 2008, no head coach in the NFL won more games than the Broncos' Mike Shanahan. After taking over on the sidelines for Denver in 1995, it took this personable yet highly disciplined leader only two years to bring a Super Bowl title to the Mile-High City. Using a run-focused variation on the "West Coast Offense" that he helped to develop as an offensive coordinator with the San Francisco 49ers, Shanahan made the Broncos into one of the most prolific scoring teams in the history of the NFL. Although Shanahan wasn't a coach who gave the media a lot of insight into his plans or his thoughts, his openness with his team made him a popular and trusted leader in the locker room and on the sidelines. His success earned the respect of his teams as well as his peers. "Mike Shanahan is one of the best," said Mike Holmgren, head coach of the Seattle Seahawks. "Everyone knows it. He's very disciplined, very thorough. He communicates well with his players. His teams play very hard." Shanahan was fired in 2008 after the Broncos missed the playoffs for a third straight season.

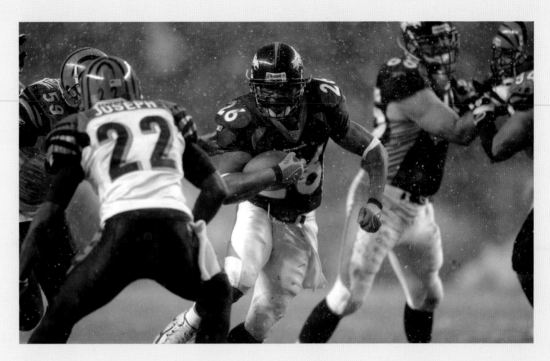

49ers. Showing veteran poise, the first-year passer led the Broncos down the field for a game-tying touchdown in the fourth quarter. But the 49ers then won in overtime, booting Denver from the playoff picture.

Just 12 hours after that loss, the Broncos received far more tragic news as young defensive back Darrent Williams was killed in a drive-by shooting early on New Year's Day. A little less than two months later, tragedy struck again as Broncos running back Damien Nash died of a heart attack while playing in a charity basketball game. There was little the team could do but look ahead to a new season while remembering their teammates. "We'll always be sad about it," said veteran safety John Lynch. "But more so, our attitude is to try and

X Denver traded halfback Tatum Bell away after he rushed for 1,025 yards in 2006, but he re-signed with the team in 2008.

X Pro Bowl linebacker Al Wilson dealt out plenty of bone-jarring tackles before a neck injury ended his NFL career in 2006.

honor these guys with the way we play and the way we live our lives."

The down times continued for the Broncos as they struggled to a 7–9 record in 2007, missing the playoffs again. Although the season was a disappointment, it provided an opportunity for Cutler to continue his development and for some other rising stars—including rookie running back Selvin Young and big wide receiver Brandon Marshall—to show their stuff. Marshall in particular was brilliant, snagging a whopping 102 catches on the year and emerging as a true star. These players and such defensive standouts as linebacker D. J. Williams kept the Mile-High City rocking

THE BRONCOS GET IT DONE

As the Broncos took the field against the Green Bay Packers after the 1997 season in Super Bowl XXXII, it was in hopes of becoming the first AFC team since the 1983 Los Angeles Raiders to become world champions. From the kickoff, the two teams traded scores as well as turnovers. At halftime, Denver led 10–7, but the Packers tied the game with a field goal early in the third quarter. The Broncos came back with a drive of their own that was highlighted by a scramble and dive by Elway to set up a first-and-goal situation. That was all Terrell Davis needed as he took the ball into the end zone on the next play. After the two teams traded touchdowns in the fourth quarter, the Packers, down 31–24, were shut down by the Broncos defense, and Super Bowl XXXII belonged to the Broncos and the AFC. Davis earned Most Valuable Player (MVP) honors as he overcame a severe migraine headache to tally 157 yards and 3 touchdowns in the game. "For all the Broncos fans who never had this feeling, we finally got it done," said Elway.

X Even though the Broncos missed the playoffs in 2006 and 2007, Invesco Field was as raucous as ever on Sunday afternoons.

RUNNING IN THE ZONE

Between 1994 and 2007, the Denver Broncos had 6 different running backs reach the 1,000-yard mark, and Terrell Davis even eclipsed the hallowed 2,000-yard barrier in 1998. Year after year, Denver running backs were among the league leaders. The reason that Denver's running game was so successful could be explained largely by a zone blocking scheme installed by offensive line coach Alex Gibbs. Instead of offensive linemen such as tackle Gary Zimmerman and center Tom Nalen locking up man-to-man with defensive players, they worked together to open up one side of the line. The running back's job was to find the first available hole and make one sharp cut through it to gain yards. The result was that running backs such as Clinton Portis (pictured) and Mike Anderson were able to waste less time waiting for their assigned hole to open up and consistently pick up positive yardage. The zone blocking scheme relied on smart, mobile linemen and running backs who could explode through the gaps. Although the Broncos made zone blocking famous, by 2008, it was used by several teams in the NFL.

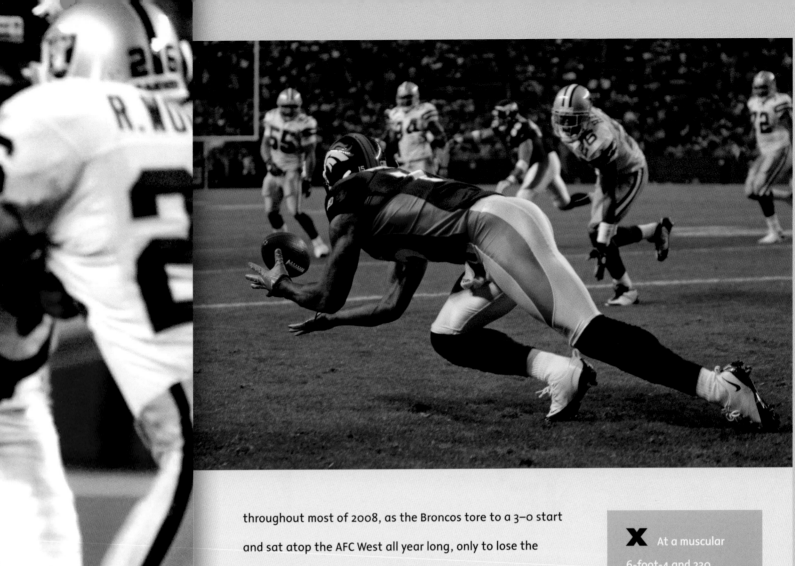

throughout most of 2008, as the Broncos tore to a 3–0 start and sat atop the AFC West all year long, only to lose the division title in the final week of the season.

The Denver Broncos have built a long and proud history in Colorado and have enjoyed their fair share of success in front of some of football's loudest and most loyal fans. From their ugly-uniform days to the Orange Crush era to the world championship teams led by John Elway, the Broncos have established themselves as one of the great football stories in the NFL. And as they continue to fight at Invesco Field at Mile High, the best may still be to come.

X At a muscular 6-foot-4 and 230 pounds, receiver Brandon Marshall was a fast-rising Broncos star nicknamed "The Beast."

INDEX